PRAYERS
FOR ANXIETY

Also by Fay Sampson:

Prayers for Dementia: And how to live well with it

Prayers for Depression: And how best to live with it

Prayers for OCD: Understanding and Healing

PRAYERS
FOR ANXIETY
And how best to cope with it

FAY SAMPSON

DARTON · LONGMAN + TODD

First published in Great Britain in 2018 by
Darton, Longman and Todd Ltd
1 Spencer Court
140–142 Wandsworth High Street
London SW18 4JJ

© 2018 Fay Sampson

The right of Fay Sampson to be identified as the Author
of this work has been asserted in accordance with the
Copyright, Designs and Patents Act 1988.

ISBN 978-0-232-53370-5

A catalogue record for this book is available from the British
Library.

www.faysampson.co.uk

Designed and produced by Judy Linard
Printed and bound in Great Britain
by Bell and Bain, Glasgow

ABOUT THIS BOOK

All of us experience anxiety at some time. It can be useful in helping us rise to a challenging situation.

For some people, the fear goes far beyond what the situation requires. Instead of sharpening our responses, it becomes disabling. This is anxiety disorder.

It's commoner than you might think. One in ten of the population will suffer from it at some point. It can have a serious effect on your life. Take heart; there are things you can do to help.

In this book you will find information and advice about different aspects of the condition: causes, symptoms, managing the illness, treatment, how others can help. Each is accompanied by a prayer.

The book is divided into two sections. Part A is for, or on behalf of, those with anxiety disorder. Part B is for family, friends and the wider community.

I have used terms like 'the one you love' and

'they'. You may wish to substitute a personal name, or the pronoun 'he' or 'she'.

At the end you will find a list of resources. I am deeply indebted to these organizations for their help, and to the many people with anxiety disorder who have described their experiences.

Half the royalties from this book will go to the charity Mind.

There are also blank pages where you may wish to add prayers you have written or discovered for yourself, and notes of other resources you have found useful.

Peace I leave with you;
my peace I give to you.

John 14:27

PART A

For the use of, or on behalf of,
those with anxiety disorder

ANXIETY

Anxiety can be good.

You need to be keyed up before an exam, a job interview or performing in public to hit the top of your ability. If you are too laid back, the result can be lack-lustre.

Anxiety becomes a disorder when the symptoms are out of proportion to the cause and the resulting condition is disabling.

You may find yourself shaking uncontrollably. Your heart is racing and you are breathing too fast. You are afraid to go out, because you fear others are watching to see you fail or make a fool of yourself. You are too tensed up to eat. You have panic attacks, and are then afraid of another attack. You can't sleep.

When you are in the middle of anxiety, it can feel as if there is no way out. It can make you feel unworthy, a failure.

Take courage. Anxiety is an illness, just as much as a physical condition like anaemia. There are things you can do to help yourself, and there are healthcare professionals who can treat you. You can find ways to cope and lead a normal life.

But it's still a frightening condition. This book explores ways to help.

Christ the Healer,

You know how desperate I feel. My life is falling to pieces. I can't control my anxiety. The world has become a hostile place.

I feel so shut in, as though others are laughing at me and judging me. Comfort me with your presence and your loving arms.

I bless you that you reach out to take me by the hand. Assure me that this is not my failure, that I am genuinely ill.

I marvel at the Gospel story which tells me that I am uniquely precious in your sight. You love me and value me enough to die for me. Help me to take the first few faltering steps to begin to believe in myself again. Guide me out of the wilderness I find myself in and back to a normal life.

A HOSTILE WORLD

Anxiety disorder distorts the way we see the world. Things that other people take in their stride seem threatening to us. We feel that we are losing friends, that we don't measure up to others' standards.

Anxiety destroys our confidence in ourselves. We fear they may be right.

The cause may lie back in childhood. If those who brought us up saw the world as dangerous, even hostile, they may have passed on that fear.

We may have been bullied, verbally or physically. That fear can carry over into later life.

There is no quick-fix way to turn your outlook around, but there are steps you can take.

Seek out a friend who has a sunnier disposition, whom you can trust. Confide in them how you feel. If they are a good friend, they will take you under their wing and stand beside you as you face the world. You may find yourself sharing a little of their optimism. You will feel less afraid to go out. Some of the warmth they evoke in others may rub off on you.

Play music and enjoy art and nature that makes you feel happier. Allow some sunshine into your life.

Friend of the Friendless,

The world seems such a hostile place that I feel my stomach screwing up when I go outside. I've lost all confidence in myself. I'm anxious about every small encounter. I'm afraid to pick up the phone.

You led your disciples through popularity and rejection. All that mattered to you was that you were pleasing in your Father's sight. Fill me with the same courage. May I no longer fear what people think of me.

Help me to raise my eyes above my own situation and concentrate on living out your kingdom. Assure me of the deep love of our Father, which never fails.

You were sensitive to the loner, the outsider. You saw the despised Zacchaeus watching from a tree, and invited yourself to his house.

Reach out to me, in all my feelings of unworthiness. Smile on me and remind me how deeply I am loved.

PANIC ATTACKS

We have an inbuilt 'fight or flight' reaction to danger. Hormones are released that make our hearts beat faster and our breathing quicken. Taken to extremes, this can develop into a panic attack. We feel faint. Our limbs turn to jelly. We either can't breathe, or we hyperventilate.

Added to the fear which triggered this, we now fear we're going to die.

Understanding your anxiety can be part of the solution. Can you recognize situations that are likely to cause a panic attack? If so, you can prepare yourself by paying attention to breathing and relaxation.

But it may happen at random. It's quite common to have a panic attack when you are asleep. You wake up soaked with sweat and panting.

Tell yourself that panic attacks may be frightening, but they only last a short time – about five to twenty minutes, usually peaking after ten. This can seem like an eternity if you are afraid you are going to die, but tell yourself it *will* pass.

Once you have had a panic attack, you will be afraid of another one.

There are routines which can prepare you: breathing exercises, relaxation techniques.

It always helps to talk to someone.

Christ, my help in danger,

I'm terrified. It doesn't matter that the terror has no real reason. I still feel as though I am going to die.

Take me by the hand. Let me feel your reassuring presence very close. Stay with me while the panicked minutes drag by. Assure me that they will end.

Lord, I'm afraid to sleep in case I wake up in a panic. May your comforting Spirit soothe me. Help me to remember those things that make me relax. Ease my tense muscles. Calm my breathing. Fill me with pleasant thoughts.

I need help. Guide me to people who will listen with understanding. Give me courage to seek my doctor's help.

It feels as if I am walking through the shadow of death. Walk beside me, precious Lord.

MEDICATION

If anxiety is disabling your life, you need to see your doctor. This is an illness that needs to be treated.

The best treatment is talking therapy. A trained therapist helps you understand the cause of your anxiety and how to manage it. Waiting lists can be long. Private treatment is available if you can afford it.

You may be prescribed medication, such as antidepressants, beta-blockers, tranquillisers. But these are only temporary reliefs. They do not address the cause of your anxiety.

Antidepressants may help you feel calmer, and more receptive to other treatment. Yet they can have side effects and even make you more anxious.

Beta-blockers can help physical symptoms like palpitations and shaking. They may help in particular stressful situations, like fear of flying.

Tranquillisers do what they say, but they carry the risk of addiction.

Pregabalin is an anti-convulsant drug occasionally prescribed.

None of these drugs will get to the root of your anxiety, but may give you help while you undergo other treatment.

You can ask your doctor about prescribing self-help resources, like exercise with a qualified trainer. You can follow many of these up yourself. Some are listed at the end of this book.

Christ my Healer,

I come to you sick in spirit. You don't need me to tell you how anxiety is disabling my life. Reach out your loving hand and guide me to where I can find help.

You know how my anxiety makes me feel unworthy, that it is somehow all my fault. Comfort me with your wisdom. Convince me that this as a genuine illness. Lead me to those who are qualified to offer healing.

Grant me patience as I wait for talking treatment. Save me from sinking into despair that nothing can help.

May I accept the offer of medication, but understand that this is not a cure. Accept my gratitude for the temporary relief it brings.

Give me the resolve to seek out resources for self-help and the energy to co-operate with my own healing.

Loving Lord, it sometimes feels as though you are the only one who believes in me. Show me that others care, that together we can find a path out of my anxiety.

BREATHLESSNESS

Mind and body are not separate. A disturbance in the mind can produce bodily symptoms. The way we treat our body affects our mood.

A common symptom of anxiety is difficulty in breathing. This can be frightening. Your chest feels so constricted that you may think you are going to die. Or you may hyperventilate, when your breathing races out of control. It can lead to dizziness and heightened blood pressure. This intensifies the feeling of panic that brought on the symptoms.

It helps to make a conscious effort to breathe deeply and slowly. This sends a message to your brain to relax. The increased oxygen will increase your sense of wellbeing.

Find out about breathing exercises, and practice them daily. Use this technique when you feel a panic attack coming on.

You may find it helpful to investigate other means of relaxation. Mindfulness, meditation and yoga are good examples. They will ease your spirit and make you feel more in control of your body.

And never underestimate the peace that comes through prayer.

Suffering Christ,

I'm desperate. I bring to you a body which seems out of control. The world already seems a threatening place, and then I find I can't breathe. My heart is racing. I'm terrified.

I feel as though no one else can possibly imagine how I'm feeling.

And then a picture comes into my mind.

You are kneeling in the Garden of Gethsemane and the sweat is rolling off you like drops of blood. You see the cross on Calvary and you are terrified.

I am humbled. You went ahead to meet the thing you feared. And now you reach back your hand to take hold of mine.

I know from the pressure of your grip that you understand the fear I feel. You will not leave me. You will walk through this with me. The simple thought of you begins to slow my breathing.

Help me to cooperate with the things that will bring my panicked body under control.

Breath of God, breathe your peace into me.

BREATHING

It's common in an anxiety attack to feel that you can't breathe, or that you are hyperventilating. You're scared you can't get enough oxygen. Really, you are getting too much. This makes you feel giddy and numb. You have chest pains. You're sweating. You think you are going to faint.

Controlling your breathing will have a huge effect on your anxiety.

Let your shoulders relax. Draw your breaths from deep inside you, from your diaphragm, not your chest. Breathe in through your nose. Let each breath out slowly through your mouth. You may start with a count of four. With practice, aim for seven counts in, eleven counts out. Your body will respond by relaxing further.

Practice this daily. You can do it standing, sitting, or lying on your back.

Loosen any tight clothing. Make yourself comfortable. Place your feet a hip-width apart.

Breathe deeply and slowly for up to five minutes.

Use this technique whenever you feel your anxiety mounting. You can also pay attention to good breathing throughout the day, until it becomes second nature.

You will find that it lowers your heart rate and blood pressure, relieves tense muscles and calms your mind.

Holy Spirit, Breath of Life,

You know how panicked I feel when I can't draw enough breath. If I was anxious before, it's worse now. I think I'm going to faint. I may even die.

Breathe deeply inside me. Let me relax my anxious body into your care. Guide me to remember the techniques I've learned. Let me concentrate on deep, slow breathing. May I feel the peace that comes as my muscles begin to loosen and a sense of well-being creeps back into my mind.

Protecting Spirit, guard me against the fear of these attacks. Help me to deal with the deeper anxiety that brings them on.

Grant me the deep-seated peace that comes when I surrender my body into your hands.

HEARTBEAT

Another common symptom of anxiety is a pounding heartbeat. This can be frightening, as if you weren't already anxious enough. You fear something is seriously wrong. You're afraid you are having a heart attack.

Ask your doctor to check that there is no physical problem with your heart. The likelihood is that this is a natural symptom of anxiety. If you can bring that under control, then the racing heartbeat will go too. Tell your doctor about this larger problem. You may be prescribed treatments to help.

Assure yourself that the pounding heartbeat may feel like a heart attack, but it isn't.

There are things you can do when you feel the symptoms coming on.

A racing heartbeat is often associated with difficulty in breathing or hyperventilation. Learning to breathe deeply and slowly can be a tremendous help.

Your body will respond positively if you go for a walk. This helps to steady your pulse and your breathing.

It may help to call a friend for reassurance during an attack. You will be less frightened of being taken ill alone.

Panic attacks begin to subside naturally after ten minutes or so. Tell yourself you only have to get through that amount of time.

Lord of the Loving Heart,

You know how often my heart goes racing out of control. I'm frightened there is something very wrong with me. I'm going to die.

Place your steadying hand upon my shoulder. Talk to me in calm tones of commonsense. Part of my brain knows that this is just a symptom of my anxiety. My body doesn't feel like that.

Help me to take control of my body and mind. May your Spirit dwell within me, calming my fears. Remind me how to control my breathing. Let me feel my whole body relax under your reassurance.

Strengthen my will to do everything I can to heal my anxiety and to practise those things that will help me relax.

You have given me a life to lead and a service to do for you. Steady my heart that I may be a useful disciple of your kingdom.

Heal my fears and calm my anxious heart.

RELAXATION

Relaxation is the antithesis of anxiety. When we are anxious, our muscles tense up, our breathing and heartbeat quicken.

Body and mind are integrated parts of ourselves. Our mood affects our body; what we do with our body can change our mood.

There are many ways to improve our relaxation: mindfulness, meditation, yoga and, of course, prayer. You may attend a class, or practise this on your own.

Choose a time and place where you won't be interrupted.

Sit or lie comfortably, with your feet on the floor and your back straight. Close your eyes or focus on something in the distance.

First, screw up your muscles. Start with your toes. Hold that position, then release it. Feel the difference? Tense as you take a deep breath in, relax as you let it out.

Move up your body, one set of muscles at a time. Make a note of any part which is harder to relax. Spend a little longer on this.

After you have reached your head muscles, relax your body completely.

Begin to move again gently. Don't rush it. Stand up slowly. Can you feel the benefit?

Do this daily. When panic approaches, consciously relax your body.

God of Peace,

You know how often the body you gave me gets out of control. I feel my muscles tensing. I break out in a sweat. I start to shake.

Surround me with your deep assurance that I am in your hands. Soothe my fears with the knowledge that there are things I can do for the symptoms that frighten me.

Grant me perseverance as I seek to bring my body and thoughts into harmony. Convince me of the importance of setting time aside each day to practice relaxing. I give you thanks that I can feel the difference.

Be the voice of calm that speaks inside me when the world seems threatening. Give me the grace to recall how to relax.

Your Son could not do what he did for us without that daily encounter with you. Grant me the deeper peace which comes from sharing my difficulties with you. May I trust myself to let go into your loving arms.

GENERALISED ANXIETY DISORDER

Anxiety may have a specific cause. We may worry about work, about money, about a new situation. Part of the cure can lie in finding strategies to cope with that problem.

Others suffer from generalised anxiety disorder. You worry about a lot of things, but there is no single cause. It goes on all day. It wakes you up at night. You get anxious about your anxiety.

It's common in generalized anxiety disorder to fear the unknown. Find out beforehand as much as you can about what to expect in new situations, either online or from friends. It helps to have someone accompany you if you are going to face something unfamiliar.

Tell yourself there is no need to perform perfectly.

Take time out, perhaps before bed, to re-order your troubled thoughts. Avoid listening to, watching or reading things which provoke negative reactions. Listen to relaxing music. Recall a pleasant memory. Dwell on the details of that happiness.

Seek out those friends who make you feel better.

There are things you can do to help you relax. But they are unlikely to be enough. If there is no one cause for your anxiety, you need to consult a doctor. This common, disabling problem is best tackled by a trained therapist.

Prince of Peace,

You know how far my life is from the rich and fruitful pattern you would wish. My anxiety is crippling me. It's making my home a prison. I'm sometimes afraid to pick up the phone.

People tell me that I am worrying about nothing. My head knows that's true. I'm fearful about things that may never happen, about situations that other people take for granted.

Only you understand that, though the cause may not be real, the fear is. You promised to walk beside me along the darkest road. Give me a powerful sense of your reassuring presence as I go towards what I fear.

Grant me the humility to seek out friends who can help me. Those who will accept my fears and stand by me.

Give me the wisdom to realize that this is a genuine illness and to seek the medical help available.

Bless me with your hope that life does not have to be like this.

TALKING

There are few mental health conditions which are not helped by sharing them. You may be afraid to talk about your anxiety in case people think less of you. If you do talk about it, you are likely to find that anxiety is commoner than you realize.

Friends and family can give you the reassurance that you lack. They may offer to accompany you in situations you find difficult. They may assure you that you stand higher in people's esteem than you feared. If your anxiety has a practical cause, they may suggest ways out.

If your anxiety is seriously disabling, you need professional talking therapy. Consult your doctor. You may have to wait a while for a referral, but it's the best cure.

Remember, there are many more who suffer as you do. If you join a group to talk about anxiety, you will be able to help other people as well as yourself. The mere knowledge that you are not the only one who experiences shaking, panic attacks, palpitations can be a help.

Talking about your anxiety is a way of bringing it under control. So is recording your symptoms in a notebook. It's easier to deal with something that is out in the open.

Healing Christ, who sought out troubled people,

I bring my fearful self before you. My anxiety wraps me round, cutting me off from my friends and family. I fear that no one else can understand. Lift me out of that self-absorption, I beg. Give me the grace to take the love that is offered to me.

Comfort me with the knowledge that help is available. Give me the courage to confess how I feel to other people.

Show me the many others who suffer as I do. May I reach out and offer a listening ear to them, and accept with thanks the support they give to me.

I thank you for the wisdom of professionals who spend their lives talking to people like me. I cannot cope with my anxiety alone. Lead me to someone who can.

In the dark night that surrounds me, walk beside me and listen to my fears.

WORRY

It is typical of anxiety disorder that you can't get your mind off what is worrying you. Friends tell you that you are getting things out of proportion. You should lighten up. But you can't.

You feel that things will get worse if you don't worry about them.

It can help to set aside a 'worry time' each day — well before bedtime. Sit down and make a list of what is worrying you. Be honest: is your fear real or imaginary? If it's real, can you solve it? Write down practical things you could do. Then, if those thoughts overtake you at other times of day, tell yourself you will attend to them in your 'worry time'.

Another thing you can do is to give your fretful mind something else to think about. Sort out those clothes, books, photographs you always meant to get under control. Volunteer to help a charity with time, money or letter-writing and follow their work. Enjoy a hobby like gardening.

Make time for music, exercise, creative activity that helps you feel more peaceful.

Accept that you have stressful emotions. You worry about some things which may not happen. Understanding yourself can keep it in proportion.

Christ, who bore the world's cares upon your shoulders,

Part of my mind knows that my worries are out of proportion. But I can't stop them chasing round my head, like a mouse looking for a hole to escape. I bring my helplessness and my anxiety to you.

Speak to me with the Spirit's calmness. Grant me courage to face up to those worries that have a real base. Shine your light of wisdom upon them. Help me to identify the steps I can take to improve things.

Give me the sense to sort out the fears that may never happen, and to decide what to do if they occur.

Save me from worrying about my worrying.

You retreated to lonely places to see the way ahead more clearly and to draw on your Father's strength. Bless me as I set aside a time to think more clearly about what worries me. Give me permission to name my fears.

May I always turn to you for strength, loving Lord.

NOTEBOOK

Anxiety makes you feel that your life is out of control. You fear that the problems are mounting up: work, relationships, health, money. You just don't know how you are going to cope.

It helps to face up to the situation, to see just what decisions you need to make. A notebook can be a great ally.

Write down all the things that are troubling you. Some of them may be real, like getting into debt. Others are 'What if?' problems, like 'What if I get cancer?'

Once you have made a list of what your worries are, you can see more clearly how to cope with them. With money problems, for instance, it might help to go to Citizens Advice. Health worries may be cleared up by a visit to your doctor. Even if your fears are groundless, it allows you to confess your anxiety problem. Your doctor should be able to help.

The notebook allows you to record what steps you have taken, and what was the result.

You can keep an informal diary, or use the sheets on the CEDAR project, 'Dealing with Worry', listed on the Resources page.

Ordering your thoughts lessens anxiety.

Great God, who ordered the universe,

Grant me the grace to take control of my messy and anxious life.

Help me not to wallow in my anxieties and say that nothing can help. You see your world in its entirety. Guide me to face the fears that are crowding in on me and put them in their proper place.

Set before me a notebook and a pen. Help me to confess what it is that I fear. Let me face the ogres of my anxiety, one by one. Show me the steps I can take, however small, to diminish them. Strengthen my resolve as I take those steps.

May I feel the comfort and reassurance of taking back control

Once I have those anxieties set down on the page, show me that there is a life beyond them. May I not reject the beauty and joy of your creation and focus only on the negatives. Grant me the grace and gratitude to rejoice in the rest of life.

STRESS

Anxiety is a natural reaction to situations of stress. The modern world presents us with plenty of these.

You may be in a job you find challenging. You may have family responsibilities that weigh heavily on you. You may have money problems. You may worry about your health.

Many of these pressures are real. No one is going to wave a magic wand and make them go away. What you can do is to prepare yourself to be more resilient.

If possible, find someone to share the things which cause you stress. Can they suggest how to ease the burden?

Being under stress doesn't mean that you are a failure. It does mean that you need to look after your physical and mental well-being.

There are simple things you can do. Looking after your body eases stress. Eat a nutritious diet. Avoid reliance on alcohol or drugs.

Be mindful of your body. Whenever you think about it, relax your muscles: neck, shoulders and so on. Smile. It does actually make you feel happier. Pay attention to deep breathing.

Find out about relaxation techniques. Perhaps join a class. Practice them daily.

Remember the One you can always lean on.

Lord of Calm,

You were besieged by crowds from morning to night. Enemies laid traps for you. Yet you found a deep reserve of calm and strength to do your Father's work.

Grant me something of that stillness. Hold my hand and ease the fear that I will not be able to cope.

You found the peace you needed in the early hours in the wilderness or by the lakeside. Strengthen me to make the time and space I need to build my own resources.

May your Spirit dwell in me, facing my fears alongside me. Help me to tread the difficult path, one step at a time, and not to be overwhelmed by it all.

Grant me the wisdom to look for ways to lighten the burden. May I not be too proud to ask for help.

When the task sometimes seems impossible, encourage me with your smile.

CREATIVITY

Creative people are often those who experience anxiety most. The psychiatrist Rollo May says, 'real creativity is not possible without anxiety'.

Conversely, many people find that creative activity helps them to manage their anxiety.

Anxiety disorder is a lonely condition. Other people don't understand how you feel. Expressing yourself through creative work can be as helpful as talking about it.

Use whatever form of art you enjoy: painting, music, writing. Don't worry about producing a perfect work. Just express what you feel inside you.

If you are one of the many creative artists who experience anxiety, it may help to choose a different art form as therapy.

Relax. Pick up the brush, the pen, the instrument and let yourself go. Don't predetermine what you are going to do. Squiggle, scribble, strum whatever comes into your head. If something more structured starts to take shape, go with it.

You may find that what you have done is a true expression of your anxiety. It may help you to understand and put a distance between yourself and your fear. Or the results may just be playful. If you enjoy it, the joy is doing you good.

Creator God,

I look at the wonders of your creation and I marvel. Yet I know that your creation often causes you pain.

Take me as I am, gripped tight in anxiety. Lay your healing hand upon me. Bless me with the freedom to explore my feelings in creative ways.

Give me joy in expressing myself. May I find a way to release what troubles me. Lift the burden from me during this space

Save me from turning my art into another reason for anxiety. Take from me the need to achieve perfection. May this be a time for release and enjoyment.

Let me give myself permission to have fun.

As I create, however inadequately, may I feel myself sharing in your great loving work.

SLEEP

Anxiety commonly makes it difficult to sleep. Worries race around your mind and won't let you relax. Lack of sleep leaves you tired next morning and less able to cope. The worries mount up. You worry now about not being able to sleep.

It helps to have a routine. Choose a bedtime when you will be ready to sleep. Avoid bright screens beforehand. Choose something relaxing instead. Keep off stimulating foods like caffeine, alcohol and sugar.

Use relaxation and breathing techniques to calm you. Take some physical exercise during the day. Hand yourself over to God in a bedtime prayer.

You may find a sleep diary helps. Note when you sleep and for how long, the quality of your sleep, whether you had nightmares. What might be contributory factors beforehand? Understanding your sleep patterns is a step towards regaining control.

You may wake up at night, sweating, your heart racing. It's best to get up. Ignore your computer or phone. Have a snack. Avoid stimulating foods. Do some of those breathing and relaxation exercises. Make a note of this in your sleep diary. When you feel ready, go back to bed. Visualise something pleasant and let your body relax.

Christ my Refuge,

You slept calmly in a fishing boat while the storm raged around you.

You know how I long for a good night's sleep. How I need it. It's not enough that my days are full of worry; my fears chase me endlessly through the night. I dread the thought that I won't be able to sleep.

Lay your calming hand upon my shoulder. Remind me of all the things that will slow my body and mind. May the breath of your Spirit help me to deepen and slow my own breathing. May the assurance of your love help me to relax each muscle. Take away the things that distract and oppress me: the computer, the phone. Fill my mind with images of beauty and peace. May your comforting presence surround me.

I wake in a panic, after too little sleep. May I know instantly that you are beside me. Your friends slept while you agonized in Gethsemane, but you will never leave me to bear this alone.

FOOD AND DRINK

What we eat and drink affects our mood.

If we're anxious, it seems natural to seek relief in alcohol, a slice of cake or a cup of well-brewed coffee. Sadly, these may actually make the condition worse.

Avoid sudden surges and dips in your blood sugar. High on the list of foods to avoid are caffeinated drinks, alcohol and sweet foods. If you really can't go the whole day without one of these, consume it well before bedtime. Stay off processed food like sausages. Avoid additives.

Instead, eat foods which release their nutrients slowly: oats, wholegrains, nuts and seeds. Choose wholemeal bread.

However churned up you feel, don't miss breakfast. Try eating little and often, rather than a couple of large meals.

So, are there foods that give positive help? Foods rich in vitamin B help. Getting your five a day of fruit and veg is essential. Oily fish, like salmon or tuna, is another good choice. So is lean beef and fermented foods like yoghurt and sauerkraut.

Plan your meals ahead. Keep the right sort of food in the house. Make a note of anything which has a bad effect on your anxiety and avoid that in future.

Lord of Plentiful Generosity,

You know how often I feel so tensed up I can't eat. You understand why I reach for a glass of alcohol or a self-indulgent cake.

Give me a vision of my body as a house for the indwelling of your Spirit. Help me understand how what I eat and drink has a positive or negative effect on my mood.

I feel that the world is against me. The last thing I want to do is to be tough with myself. I stand in awe of the discipline that drove you to fast in the wilderness. Give me just a little of that courage to take my future into my own hands. May I do what I can to cooperate with my own well-being.

You came back from the wilderness to enjoy food with friends and strangers. You were a popular guest at their tables. I ask you to give me back the simple pleasure in good food, that will calm my mood.

MONEY

Money, or the lack of it, is a frequent cause of anxiety. If you are struggling to make ends meet, an unexpected bill can throw you into debt. You may be tempted to cheer yourself by buying yourself something nice or find solace in alcohol. You use your credit card. The debts mount. When you see your next bill, you feel sick. Severe anxiety can make you unable to work.

It's hard to see a way out. Anxiety stops you thinking clearly.

It helps to take a good look at the problem. Sit down and make an assessment of your finances: income, expenditure, debts, savings.

Is there a way to economise? Could you save by making more of your own meals? Cut down on alcohol? Spend less on clothes? Walk more? It will depend on your individual lifestyle. Make a plan. Repeat the exercise next month. Can you see a difference?

It helps to have savings for that unexpected bill. Set up a standing order to put a little of your income aside. It may be hard, but it will give you reassurance.

If your debts seem unmanageable, go to Citizens Advice.

Anxiety is eased when you take control.

Generous God, who clothes the wild flowers in glory,

I beg you to lift from me my crushing anxiety about my finances. I'm in debt, and I can't see a way out. I worry about things that could happen that I wouldn't have enough money to cope with.

I struggle with an inadequate income. Show me how to make what little I have go further. May I have the humility to ask for help in freeing myself from debt.

You understand how tempting it is to use a credit card for things I can't afford. Strengthen my resolve to live within my means, even if that stops me buying expensive presents for the people I love.

My hardships are real. Give me the grace not to make them worse by worrying about things that may not happen. You showed us how the wild birds are fed, and the flowers clothed. Grant me your blessed assurance to get through one day at a time.

STUDENTS

The impression is that students have a great time at university. Many do. But a sizeable number find the reality difficult to cope with.

You're away from home for the first time. You've lost your support network. Others are making friends, partying, coping with the new work. You feel left out in the cold. You're finding university work a challenge. You're afraid you won't be able to keep up.

Your anxiety mounts. Faced with the demands, you feel sick and start to shake.

There are hundreds of others who feel as you do. The pressures of university life are real.

That's why there is a network of support. If you find it hard to cope, go to your personal tutor, a campus counsellor, one of the chaplains. Talking about your problems is a good first step to managing them.

If academic work is stressful, take time to understand what you are taught. Go over your notes and the marking of assignments. Mark the difficult bits. Check things out with fellow-students. Ask your tutor for help.

Take regular exercise. Pay attention to your diet. Practice breathing and relaxation. Make a timetable that allows you enough time for study, relaxation and sleep.

Shepherd of the Lost Sheep,

I so looked forward to going to university. Now I feel I'm out of my depth. I thought I would make friends, but I find myself in my room alone.

The teaching's different. I feel I've been thrown into the deep end. I'm afraid I'll sink.

Be the Lifeguard who grips me and tows me to safety. Calm my panic. Teach me to control my anxious body.

Nicodemus sought you out at night to talk to you. May I too learn how talking can help me manage. May I not be ashamed to seek the help that is offered.

You divided your time between solitary prayer and hectic activity. Help me manage my days. Let me give my studies the time they need, and not run away from difficulties. Give me back the joy of studying.

When I feel left out, give me the grace to look for someone else on the fringes. May I offer the hand of friendship that will help both of us.

EXERCISE

There is a strong connection between our mind and body. Anxiety causes a number of physical symptoms: nausea, dizziness, difficulty breathing and many more. Conversely, what we do with our bodies affects our minds. The act of smiling makes us feel happier.

If you suffer from anxiety disorder, you can use this to improve your condition. Even playing with a worry ball in a stressful situation can help.

Better still, take regular exercise, preferably outdoors. It can be walking, running, cycling, tai chi — whatever you will most enjoy. You will come away feeling more refreshed and relaxed. It helps you to eat and sleep better. It benefits your breathing.

Even if it's only fifteen minutes indoors, build it into your day and stick to it. Perhaps do more at the weekend.

The early morning is the best time, but not the only one. Think about using your lunch break for a brisk walk and a picnic outdoors.

Physical exercise releases endorphins in the brain. These are feel-good chemicals which help you to relax and sleep. More vigorous exercise creates a beneficial effect for hours.

Regular exercise requires an effort of will. Choose an accountability partner to keep you up to scratch.

Christ who walked the hills of Palestine,

I place my anxious body in your hands.

You know how often my heart and breathing seem out of control. I'm afraid I'll faint. Give me your assurance that there are ways to overcome this.

You understand how weak I am when it comes to exercise. You know I'll make excuses about lack of time and inclination. You disciplined your life in order to serve us. Strengthen my own will to make my body fit to serve you better. Let me feel the benefit in both body and mind.

So much about the world seems hostile. I bless you for the enjoyment that comes from activity in the fresh air. May I rejoice in the sun, the wind, even the rain. Let me feel my muscles growing stronger, my breathing deepening, my body relaxing healthfully.

As the feel-good chemicals are released in my tensed-up body, so may your Spirit flow through my soul bringing a deeper peace.

SOCIAL MEDIA

Nowadays, we have a multitude of ways to keep in touch with our friends, to share news and pictures. But this freedom also carries risks.

Most young people care about being popular. They are afraid they won't measure up in looks or prowess. It's very easy for someone thoughtless or cruel to post something that undermines that shaky confidence.

You may worry that you don't have as many 'friends' as other people. When you have posted or tweeted something, you have to keep checking for 'likes' and responses. This can lead to very real feelings of anxiety. Stress increases with the size of your network.

Try taking your input less seriously. Don't constantly fret about which picture to post or the best words to use. Ration yourself to a minute or two to decide. The likelihood is that your friends won't treat you any differently if you are less obsessive.

Social networking can become an addiction, affecting the brain like cocaine. Give yourself an occasional break. You may be constantly on your phone. Put it away for a while. Concentrate instead on the world around you.

Social media can be good. Don't let it take over your life.

Christ, my closest Friend,

People cheered when you rode into Jerusalem; they shouted 'Crucify!' when you stood before Pilate. May I know myself so securely loved by you that my life does not depend on the number of 'friends' or 'likes'.

I want to be popular. I don't have the strength to stand on my own. Surround me with your lasting friendship.

Grant me the compassion to understand that others feel like me. Give me the grace to pay attention to others on the margins of popularity. May I encourage them and respond positively to their posts.

Take me away for times of respite, as you withdrew from the crowds. Instil in me the discipline to mark out times free from social media. Help me to put away my phone. Open my eyes to your glorious world around me. Make me thankful to be alive in the here and now.

Give me the grace and humility to accept myself as I am. Allow me to forgive myself my imperfections.

PART B

For the use of family, friends
and the wider community

SUPPORT

You notice that someone you care about is not coping well with life. They are not eating properly. They don't seem to be enjoying themselves. They look tired.

Talk to them. You may find that they are suffering from undue anxiety. Listen patiently. Take their anxiety seriously. Don't tell them there is no need for it. It is part of the disorder that the symptoms are out of proportion to the cause.

Do what you can to boost their self-esteem. They probably feel that the world is hostile to them. Foster a genuine appreciation of their own worth.

There may be practical problems: pressure at work, money difficulties, a new and challenging situation. Encourage them to talk about this, in confidence. You may be able to make some suggestions, but don't offer glib solutions. It's better if talking itself helps them towards coping with their anxiety.

If the condition is seriously disabling, suggest that they visit their doctor. There is medication and, better still, talking therapy which can help.

Find out all you can about anxiety. www.mind. org.uk is a good place to start.

Introduce to them to this advice when you feel they are ready to move on.

Friend of the Friendless,

I bring before you the one I care about. I know that they are suffering a dark night of anxiety. Reach out your loving arms to them. Use me to help.

Grant me the wisdom to listen more than I talk. Let the out-welling of their suffering be the beginning of their healing.

Give me the grace to take seriously the symptoms they tell me of: the sweating, the nausea, the panic attacks. Let me assure them that I am there for them, that I will support them with my presence when I can, and always with my prayers.

You chose a despised tax-collector to be your apostle. Let me raise the self-esteem of the one I care about. May I help them see themselves as you see them, uniquely valued. Let me influence others to do the same.

Help me to find out all I can about ways to healing, or simply coping with these symptoms. Guide us both to those who can help them best.

FRIENDS

Social media can be a source of enjoyment and connectivity. We appreciate seeing the 'likes' multiply for our posts. The number of our 'friends' and 'followers' mounts.

For others it may be the opposite. People post hurtful things, carelessly or deliberately. Few want to follow or befriend them. In our social-media orientated world this can cause serious stress. That person feels devalued, unlikeable.

If someone you know is showing signs of anxiety and there is no other obvious cause, bring up the subject of social media.

If this is the cause of their worry, take steps to help. Resolve to follow your friend's posts and express support. Encourage others to do the same. You may want to suggest things your friend could post about which will attract 'likes'. Cyber-bullying should be reported.

It's a delicate matter, but you may want to advise them to spend less time on social media. Anxiety can make people retreat into their shell, where their computer, tablet, or phone is their only connection to the outside world.

Invite them out. Give them a good time. Be generous with your praise about their appearance and achievements.

Agree that you too will take a break from social media.

Lord of the Lonely,

I bring to you my friend who is stressed by social media. You know it has left them feeling unworthy and unloved. Make me the good friend they need. Show me how I can support them, both online and in other ways.

May I use what influence I have to rally friends around them. Show us how to do everything we can to raise their self-esteem. Make us quick to counter anyone who posts hurtful things. Make us generous in our own responses.

Grant me the wisdom to help my friend find enjoyment in other ways. Guard us both against over-dependence on social media. Help me to take a day off now and then, and to strengthen the resolve of my friend to do the same.

Anxiety strikes deep into the foundations of people's confidence. You know how to bring them inner peace. Watch over my friend, and me. Grant us both the deep assurance which comes from knowing that we are uniquely loved and precious.

WORK

Work gives us a sense of identity. But there can be problems.

We may have a manager who undermines our confidence in our ability to do the job. We may be faced with new tasks, and doubt our ability to cope. We may have a colleague who makes us feel uncomfortable.

If someone you are responsible for starts calling in sick, consider that the root cause may be mental rather than physical. They may be suffering from anxiety disorder.

First, you need to realize that this is a genuine illness. Have a talk, and see if there is anything worrying them. Encourage them to report their symptoms to a doctor. If it helps, delegate this conversation to someone who is a sympathetic listener.

Review your work practices. Could there be any bullying or harassment that you need to stop? If people are assigned new tasks, are they given the training to cope?

You may be a colleague of the person in distress. Don't just sit on the sidelines. Encourage them to talk about it. Respect their confidence. If you identify a problem at work, report it to someone who will help, if you can do this without compromising your friend.

Let them know they have your support.

Compassionate Christ,

Give me the same heart of compassion for those who need my help.

Make me observant of the colleagues around me. May I be sensitive to absences and concerned about the cause. Let me find a way to offer sympathetic help.

Save me from thinking that mental illness is the fault of the person concerned. May I treat it as I would any other sickness.

So far as am responsible, may I do everything I can to make the workplace a source of satisfaction and creativity. Let me support those who are finding it hard and try to make things smoother.

You called your disciples apart to refresh themselves from their labours. Show me when someone needs that respite.

If necessary, give me the courage to speak up in support of my friend. Open my eyes to harassment, bullying, undue pressure to perform. May I stand alongside a colleague suffering from anxiety, as you unfailingly stand by me.

CHILDREN

Even children in primary school suffer from anxiety. It is common among teens.

A frequent cause is the desire for popularity. Social media plays a big part. Many children feel they don't match up to those they deem more popular. They may even be the victims of cyber-bullying.

There are also the pressures of exams, a new school. A different teacher can upset a comfortable routine. A child can feel lost in a larger crowd.

If a child is reluctant to go to school, if they are off their food and seeming miserable, you need to check what is wrong. They need a sympathetic ear. Assure them that anxiety is a common condition. It's not just them. Take their fears seriously. Telling them there is really nothing to worry about is unlikely to help.

If the condition is serious, and prevents them getting on with their life, take them to see a doctor. There is medication which may provide temporary relief while the underlying problem is sorted out. There are talking therapies, which are one of best ways of treatment, though there may be a waiting list.

Let them always feel your loving care and pride in them.

Loving Father,

I'm worried about my child. I want them to have a happy childhood, but it isn't happening. They're withdrawn, unhappy to go out. They're not eating properly, and I don't think they're sleeping well.

Help me be the calm and loving parent they need. May I never forget to reassure them with a hug and a word of praise. Let me show them how much I love and value them. Let me not make unrealistic demands.

May I earn the trust that will let them talk to me. Let me take their fears seriously.

Give me wisdom to find words that will help. Show me where to learn more about anxiety and how to relieve it.

May they know that when I am troubled myself, I take my worries to you. Let me not be embarrassed to show how important you are to me. Yet save me from giving a false impression that faith is an easy answer.

Accompany us both through their fears and bring them peace.

CARING

Living with someone with anxiety disorder can be wearing. You try to be encouraging, but you're met with negativity. Their fear of going into certain situations limits your own life.

Try to imagine yourself into their situation. Don't sound judgemental. Don't try to argue them out of it. Anxiety doesn't respond to logic.

Assure them that nobody expects perfection.

There are no quick answers to anxiety disorder, but there are things that help. Read up on self-help resources. Encourage the one you love to do the same.

It's easier to shrug off advice from someone close to us. You may need to insist that they see a doctor. If necessary, accompany them for support. Make sure you know what the doctor advises.

Your own health is important too. You need times when you get out and enjoy yourself. It may seem callous to leave the one you love behind, but it's important for both of you that you hang on to the vision of normality. This is what you want your loved one to achieve.

You need that refreshment to carry on with the loving caring that you do.

You naturally feel responsible, but it's not all down to you.

Caring Father,

I feel guilty about bringing my complaints to you, when I'm not the one with anxiety disorder.

But it's getting me down. I feel as though my pockets are weighted with stones. I try to be reassuring, but it doesn't seem to work.

Give me strength enough for the two of us. May I understand the fears they suffer, even when they seem irrational. Show me the words of wisdom that will make a difference.

Help me to keep my own anxieties in check while I reassure the other that the world is not a hostile place.

Help me create a healthy lifestyle for both of us.

You knew how the pressure of the crowds weighed on your disciples. You saw to it that they had times of refreshment. In your tender mercy, give me permission to go out sometimes and enjoy myself.

Give us both the grace to forgive ourselves when we fall short.

Lead us together into the deep peace which lies in you.

CHURCH

We look round our congregation on a Sunday morning and identify certain people we need to pray for: the bereaved, those in hospital, those awaiting tests.

There are others with illnesses which have less obvious signs. It is highly probable that some of those we worship with will be suffering from serious anxiety.

We need to read up on anxiety disorder. Knowing about it can make us sensitive to signs like unexplained absences. If someone seems more withdrawn and looks tired and strained, we need to follow up on that.

This is something any one of us can do, but we can also report our concerns to the minister and pastoral workers.

People suffering from anxiety will have a lowered self-esteem. Make a point of greeting those who seem to be retiring into the shadows. Tell them we enjoy seeing them.

If you are seriously worried, you may want to invite that person to meet you for coffee and a chat. Don't press too hard, but invite them to open up. Talking is a great help. You might confess some of your own fears and weaknesses to encourage sharing.

Pray for them, whether you name them in public or not.

Father, who sees each nestling fall,

Deepen our concern for all who worship with us. May we look beyond physical illness and be aware how common mental ill-health is.

Guide us to find out more about this, so that we recognize the signs. May those who suffer from anxiety disorder know that they belong to a caring community.

In your wisdom, show us how we can help. We know that talking can be a means of healing. Guide us to find the right person to do this. Show me if this is me.

May the warmth of our welcome surround everyone who comes through our doors. Make them feel uniquely valued, as they are in your sight.

Grant that our services may be times of beauty and refreshment. Bless those who lead them to deepen the closeness those in anxiety feel to their Father.

May we be a noticing church, so that those in need find the opportunity to share their pain.

Keep us constant in prayer for those in need.

FAMILIES

Anxiety disorder doesn't just affect the person with that condition. It's a strain for anyone who lives with them. There's a constant tension. It's hard to plan a social life if one of the family is afraid to go out.

It can be particularly hard on children. They don't understand why their parent doesn't behave like other people's. Worrying that their parent is ill can make children more demanding. They need to test that their parent really can look after them.

It's hard on the partner too. At the end of a day's work, it's natural to want to turn to each other for support, for laughter, for companionship, for sex. That's hardly possible with a continuously anxious partner. More of the family burden falls on one of you.

If you see this happening to your friends, offer help, not just to the person with anxiety. You might take the children out. Give them a worry-free fun time.

You could offer the partner a listening ear, so that they can unload their frustrations and fears. If this is someone of the opposite sex, be careful not to get too involved. Perhaps ask a more appropriate person to do this.

Christ our Brother,

You opened your arms and made us your family.

Embrace the family I bring to you in prayer. The anxiety of one hangs like a cloud over all of them.

I pray for the children, living in an atmosphere of strain and fear. Let me give them the reassurance of trust in you. May their own lives not fall victim to worry because of their parent's anxiety.

Show me how to lighten the tension and give them times of happiness.

I hold before you the partner of the one with anxiety. You know the constant stress they live under, how hard it is to remain loving and reassuring, when nothing they do seems to help. Give them the support they need. Help me to see that they get a break.

May I be willing to step in and help my friend, both because they need it, and to relieve those who live with them.

Make us a noticing people, so that families in difficulty never go unsupported.

CALM

When you are close to someone with anxiety disorder it can be tempting to offer easy solutions. You reassure them there is nothing harmful in the situation they fear. You make suggestions for coping with stress at work or at home. You recommend relaxation and breathing techniques. You tell them to see a doctor.

The result may be that they huddle closer in their shell. They tell you that you don't understand. You don't know what it feels like. They can't just argue away their fear.

They're right. One of the problems with anxiety disorder is that the fears are often illogical.

Be patient and learn. Do your best to empathise. If you try to rush them into action before they're ready, it will only make them more anxious.

Start by making your times together occasions of relaxation. Visit them at home if they feel safer there. Or take them out somewhere nice but make all the decisions yourself. Think first of their pleasure.

Don't push things but let them know they can talk to you. Talking is the best healing for anxiety.

Let them know you are praying for them.

Practical advice can come later as you gain their confidence.

Above all, let taking it to God in prayer not be a clichéd response but a reality.

Spirit of Peace,

Rest your calming hand on the one I bring before you. The world crowds in upon them and they fear it. Grant me the grace to be part of your peace and healing.

Save me from rushing in with hasty answers. Let me learn to understand how this disorder feels. Give me patience when I'm itching to suggest solutions.

May my presence be a time that they look forward to. Grant me the humility to listen more than I talk.

Show me how to bring a little sunshine into their life. Let us do enjoyable things together, while freeing them from the anxiety of planning anything. May they trust me in a world that seems hostile.

I know, as you do, that there are ways for people with anxiety to cope. Grant me the wisdom to sense when the time is right for advice, and to go gently until then.

Be a friend to both of us as I help them to move forward.

RESOURCES

Mind has an excellent website, which deals with many aspects of anxiety disorder: its symptoms, causes, treatment and how to live with it as well as possible. It includes video-clips from those coping with anxiety.www.mind.org.uk.

The information is also available as booklets. Mind infoline: 0300 123 3393 and info@mind.org.uk.

The NHS provides information on anxiety and related conditions. www.nhs.uk/Conditions/Anxiety/Pages/Introduction.aspx. You can also obtain help from your local surgery.

AnxietyUK deals specifically with this condition. www.anxietyuk.org.uk. www.anxieties.com covers self-help treatments for many aspects of anxiety.

Clinical Education Development and Research (CEDAR) provides helpful worksheets on 'Dealing with Worry'. http://cedar.exeter.ac.uk/iapt/iaptworkbooksandresources.

A common feature of anxiety disorder is panic attacks. Specific advice on this can be found at www.panic-attacks.co.uk.

This is also covered by No Panic. www.nopanic. org.uk.

YouTube has many short films from people who have anxiety disorder, telling about ways they have found to cope. www.youtube.com/watch?v=SDPW3pdlnLk

This is only a selection of the help available. Most of it is free; some requires a subscription or a purchase.

These pages are left blank for your own prayers.